This notebook
belongs to

_____

Funny Office Notebooks
for smart people like you

Check out our other fun notebooks that you can use yourself or give out as gifts. And don't forget to leave a quick review.

Bored at Work • Snarky Office • Tired of Working
Corporate Ladder Guides • Executive Career Guides

Always take notes during meetings because your brain
retains less than 5% of what is said. Need another notebook?

Holland has the shortest work week in the world
with only 29 hours per week.

By the age of 40, an average American has held
seven or eight different jobs.

Nearly 60% of employees report checking their work email over Christmas and Thanksgiving.

Refrigerating rubber bands makes them last longer. Just let them adapt to the normal temperature change before stretching them too much.

Official government Occupational Safety studies have shown that taking four additional 5-minute breaks daily away from the computer will make you feel better but not reduce your work output.

Multitasking leads to increased stress, a 10% drop in IQ,
and as much as a 40% drop in productivity.

In 1968, Spencer Silver was working on creating a super strong glue.
He failed and created a weak adhesive that left no residue behind.
It took another three years to find a use for it – the Post-It note.

Reserved for Random Thoughts

The average raise is 3% but the average salary increase after switching jobs is 10-20%. Staying with the same company means earning 50% less over your lifetime than those who are strategically changing jobs.

24% of commuters say that when they are stuck in traffic, they think "deep" thoughts. What do you think about?

_____

_____

_____

_____

_____

_____

_____

_____

_____

_____

_____

_____

_____

_____

_____

_____

_____

_____

_____

_____

_____

_____

_____

_____

_____

_____

_____

_____

70% of Americans with full-time jobs are not inspired by their work or their managers. That makes them less productive and engaged at work.

King of France Louis XV was the first to use a stapler to bind his royal papers. Each staple had the insignia of the royal court and was made out of solid gold and encrusted with precious stones.

An average worker spends more than a quarter of their day reading and answering emails. If you check emails only at set times in the day, you will increase your productivity.

People who work nights are almost twice as likely to
have an accident than those who work day shifts.

A ballpoint pen has enough ink to draw a line that's two miles long.
A pencil has enough graphite to go for 35 miles! You'd need almost
half a million pens and 6,825 pencils to draw a line to the Moon.

After Monday, Friday is the second most likely day to call in sick.
I wonder why? Otherwise, Fridays are usually the day
when the office is much more positive and social.

Eighty percent of jobs are gained through networking.

More people walk or bike to work in Alaska than any other US state.

Nearly 80% of American workers are dissatisfied with their jobs.

Focused 90 minutes of work followed by a 20-minute break will make you much more productive. Also, look into "The Pomodoro Technique".

A professional typist's fingers travel 12.6 miles
during an average workday.

Laughter boosts your immune system by enhancing your antibodies and increasing your immune cell count. This helps reduce your chances of getting sick and missing out on work.

Listening to music while working actually helps people
get things done faster.

Staring at the green color can make you more creative and productive.

Reserved for Great Ideas

For maximum productivity, it's necessary that your desk is organized.

The average worker in America receives 200 email, paper,
and phone messages per day.

In a phenomenon called "karoshi," a high number of Japanese workers drop dead at their work desks due to their 60 to 70-hour workweeks. Every year, over 10,000 Japanese suffer "karoshi."

For every 1,470 resumes received, an employer will hire only one person.

The average workweek in the US is surprisingly only 34.5 hours.
But for the hardest working age range of 25-54, it is 40.3.

Charles Darwin invented the modern office chair. He added wheels to his own chair so that he could move around his office easier.

People who don't get involved in office politics are
more successful and efficient at work.

One quarter of office workers report a productivity
decrease in the summertime.

Almost 40% of young professionals in the US are so unhappy with the lack of paid parental leave that they'd be willing to move to another country because of it.

Monday is the most common sick day except in Australia.
Their most common sick day is Tuesday. G'day!

Nine out of ten Millennials are expected to change jobs
every three years. This means that most of them will have
15-20 jobs in their lifetimes.

_____

_____

_____

_____

_____

_____

_____

_____

_____

_____

_____

_____

_____

_____

_____

_____

_____

_____

_____

_____

_____

_____

_____

_____

_____

_____

_____

It's a myth that NASA spent a million dollars to develop the space pen.
The Fisher Pen Company did that on their own while creating it.
Before 1967, NASA simply used pencils in space.

Employees who work under managers who integrate humor into their interactions report experiencing greater work satisfaction.

You can revive an old permanent marker by soaking it in a bit of rubbing alcohol until the ink starts to leak. Then, put the cap on and let it dry for 15 minutes. For regular markers, use water instead.

When office temperatures are low (68F/20C), employees make 44% more errors and are less productive than when it's warmer (77F/25C).

Reserved for the Bucket List

Employees who have more control over the layout and design
of their workspace are healthier and happier at work.

Before the Pregnancy Discrimination Act in 1978, American women could actually get fired from a job for being pregnant!

People are more productive on days when they exercise before work.

More than 16% of new hires quit within their first seven days on the job. 31% quit within the first six months.

A typical work desk is home to 400 times more bacteria than
the average toilet seat. Yikes! Time to clean your desk?

Laughter can lower your heart rate, reduce your blood pressure, and boost the function of your blood vessels. It improves your blood flow which reduces your chances of cardiovascular diseases.

Once an item is filed away, there is a 98% chance
it will never be seen again. Uh-oh!

Having live plants in your work environment helps productivity.

In 1965, executive pay in the US was 20 times higher than average worker pay. Today, executive pay is around 300 times the worker pay!

Multitasking at work can drop your IQ by 10 points!
That's the equivalent of losing one night's sleep or
twice the effect of smoking marijuana.

On average, US businesses spend $250,000 per year
to cover the costs associated with employee turnover.

You would need 507,000,000 Post-It notes to circle the world once.

Bosses who integrate humor as part of their management style create greater work performance, satisfaction, and cohesion amongst workers, and are perceived as better leaders and managers.

85% of all highlighters sold are yellow. It's in the middle of the visible spectrum of light and the easiest shade for the color-blind to see.

Adults who regularly get 7.5 to 9 hours of sleep
are up to 20% more productive.

Average workweek around the world is about 45 hours long.
Those in North Korea's labor camps work over 112 hours per week!

Breathing toner particles from photocopiers and printers is as bad for the lungs as smoking. It can also irritate your eyes, nose, and lungs.

A normal-size paper can be folded in half NO more than seven times. And thanks to exponential growth, if you WERE able to fold it 42 times, your paper would reach the Moon – literally!

Happy employees are 12% more productive than others.

Reserved for Doodling

www.ingramcontent.com/pod-product-compliance
Lightning Source LLC
Chambersburg PA
CBHW071324220526

45468CB00001B/492